A Double Portion to Know Him

Knowing Who God Is in a World That Limits Him

Dr. Amber Goodman
Dr. Ashley Goodman

ISBN-13: 9798693067417

Edited by Lisa Irving of FireCopy | www.thefirecopy.com
Cover design by Vincent Irving

Library of Congress Control Number: 2018675309
Printed in the United States of America

Contents

This book is dedicated to Abba Father, our Lord Jesus Christ, and to our wonderful teacher, the Holy Spirit.

Foreword

This book is so anointed and was written by the power of the Holy Spirit. It welcomes you and allows you to experience spiritual healing and deliverance. It is an easy guide to fostering a new love and relationship with Jesus Christ. The lives of these young ladies are a testament and a testimony. I consistently have witnessed their insatiable fervor for Christ as their Overseer. I am writing this foreword because I believe in this dynamic duo. I have seen abundant manifestations in their lives time and time again, and the power of the Living God is beyond imminent in all that they do. This book is a life-changer!

I have known Drs. Amber and Ashley Goodman for a few years now. As they are now ordained Evangelists, I have watched their lives blossom in the word of God and in the work of the Lord. They live a holy life unto the Lord, they walk in God's wisdom, and in the knowledge and revelation of His Son Jesus Christ. The call of Christ Jesus and the anointing on their lives are so powerful and will be evident as you read and meditate on *A Double Portion to Know Him*.

I did not really know the Lord until I was in my thirties. My road began with some difficulties. Once I discovered how awesome a pure relationship with the Lord was, it changed my life forever. I have been in ministry now for over 27 years, and I have traveled to other continents. I oversee nine churches in the United States, one in the Philippines, and one in India. There are a plethora of pastors and licensed ministers under my tutelage locally, statewide, nationally, and internationally. I am on an incredible journey with the Master. Your journey with the Master can begin right here, right now.

Prophet Daniel Powell, Sr., Overseer
With love from Prophetess Esther Powell
Faith & Works Outreach Ministries, Int. | Heaven to Earth Worship Center

Introduction

As evangelists of our Lord and Savior Jesus Christ, we wanted to spread a message of encouragement. This book is for anyone searching for an abundance of peace, joy, and happiness. It is the foundation of the message God has given to both of us through His revelation and teachings from the Holy Spirit. It took us approximately two years to receive the full revelation of this writing. Writing lets us know the history and recordings of time, what God is doing during a specific generation through His people. It is the inspiration of the Holy Ghost using us to spread God's word throughout the earth as willing vessels. He empowers us with the pen of a ready writer like His servant, Apostle Paul, who wrote the majority of the New Testament. It is so powerful to see how his writing continues to bless millions of souls and leads souls into the kingdom of God.

In February 2018, God sent a prophet as His mouthpiece to instruct us to write a book that would assist others in learning who He is. The book would reject the popular idea of God as a distant, inaccessible presence. At the time of this prophetic word, we had no idea a book was inside of us. We had to decide if we were going to obey God or allow our self-doubts and worldly viewpoint to stop us from fulfilling this assignment. A major component of the worldly viewpoint we struggled against was the notion that most people with a mathematical or scientific background are not great writers. Now, as mature, born-again believers who are no longer babes in Christ, we know better. We understand that the Greatest Author of all time has graced us to participate in this form of evangelism in order to bless others.

The negative seed of not being skilled at writing was planted in us during our early childhood and continued throughout high school. We will explore the topic of negative seeds later, but take note that most negative seeds, demonic spirits, and generational curses, try to enter in during the early stages of one's life – childhood or early adulthood. For most of our lives, we never thought we were that great at writing, but God's grace will prepare, groom, and show you what your gifts are – no matter how limited you have allowed your mindset or capabilities to be.

To return to our writing journey, in the months leading up to our graduation from pharmacy school, we were in a state of frustration, resentment, and uneasiness about our futures. We were fulfilling the wrong wills, which consisted of our *own* wills and God's *permissive* wills for our lives. Pursuing your *own* will, or *free will*, means you depend on yourself, you do things your own way. You work so hard in your own strength to try to create and make things happen for yourself. You at times burn out from trying so hard, thinking that is the cycle of success. However, you do not have peace in everything that you do, and, from a spiritual perspective, there is no success without peace. Being in God's *permissive* will means that you did not seek His kingdom and His righteousness, but He allowed it to happen anyway.

If someone chooses her *own* will or is in God's *permissive* will for her life, she will have insufficient strength, walk in disobedience, and allow the flesh to miscarry her destiny, which all comes with the added burden of sorrow. Pursuing your *own* will or God's *permissive* will instead of God's *perfect* will result in the missing of your destiny and the unfulfillment of your calling. The impact you were meant to have on others will not happen to the magnitude you were supposed to reach. When God reveals His purpose and His calling unto you, your current logic may not be able to make sense of it. Moreover, it is often revealed to you during difficult or unpredictable times. Do not misunderstand that, as humans, we certainly can envision and have an understanding of our talents and gifts. Still, we may delay our destiny by seeking our own will and desires rather than God's perfect plan for our lives.

Therefore, the purpose of this book is to inspire and bring insight to anyone seeking God's perfect will. We discuss how to receive healing, deliverance, and restoration. We offer guidance as to how people can mature in their faith journey through our Lord and Savior Jesus Christ. We want to help people understand that their careers may not always line up with their purpose. However, in those careers, one can find the skills needed to fulfill that purpose and use it for His glory. Your career does not define who you are or what God has chosen you to be, but if your passion and purpose do align, and it gives you peace, then you are on the right path to finding true success.

This piece of knowledge is meant to bring light to those aspiring to be world-changers. Our hope is that these words of wisdom guide readers into a life of eternal peace, clarity of purpose, and courage to continue to run the race of faith until their mission is complete. If you are tired of living blindly by not knowing your destiny outside of your own consciousness, or you have felt delayed in pursuing what He has placed down on the inside of you for activation and release, recite this prayer: *Dear Lord, I pray against every twist, trap, or trick of the enemy for delaying my destiny, but God according to your timing and the Holy Spirit in me, God I pray that you release and reveal my destiny to me. Not so that I can prove my work(s), but so that I can bring glory to you. In Jesus's name, Amen.*

When we let God be God, His perfect will is easy to fulfill.

"For I know the plans I have for you," declares the Lord, "plans to prosper you and not to harm you, plans to give you hope and a future." *Jeremiah 29:11, NIV*

"Father, if you are willing, take this cup from me; yet not my will, but yours be done." *Luke 22:42 NIV*

"My people are destroyed for lack of knowledge; because you have rejected knowledge, I also will reject you from being priest for Me; Because you have forgotten the law of your God, I also will forget your children." *Hosea 4:6 NKJV*

"Now concerning spiritual *gifts,* brethren, I do not want you to be ignorant: You know that you were Gentiles, carried away to these dumb idols, however you were led.

Therefore, I make known to you that no one speaking by the Spirit of God calls Jesus accursed, and no one can say that Jesus is Lord except by the Holy Spirit." *1 Corinthians 12:1-3 NKJV*

"But seek first the kingdom of God and His righteousness, and all these things shall be added to you." *Matthew 6:33 NKJV*

Chapter I: To Know Him

To know God is the reason why His Son, Jesus Christ, came into the world as the Son of Man. Jesus Christ reconciled our relationship with our Heavenly Father who is the Creator of mankind. Despite this, many people refer to God as *a higher power*, *the universe*, *energy*, or *something told me*. Some refer to or explain Him only in terms of their trials and successes through past earthly experiences. God never called or referred to Himself as *a higher power, the universe*, *energy*, or *something told me* in the Holy Bible.

Referring to God as *a higher power* suggests that there are positions or rankings of power that are comparable to Him when there definitely are not! God stands alone. Such misleading language also causes individuals to not know the standards that Jesus Christ desires for us to follow, which are those of the One and Only true living God. Too many have become comfortable in adopting ideas and practices of false gods, legalism, cultures, witchcraft, and the religious doctrine of mankind.

We will only know who God is through studying His word and receiving sound teaching. Once we know God as Abba Father, we begin to know more about our identity and how we are truly supposed to live as His son Jesus Christ exemplified for us. Our God loves us so much so that He allowed not only His Son to be a gift to us, but He allowed Jesus to give us a teacher and counselor, the Holy Spirit, who guides us into all truth.

For those who want to know Him, a church home and a preacher are must-haves. People often assume that a preacher automatically means *a pastor*, but it does not. A preacher is an individual that holds an office in the five-fold ministry—an order that we will explain in this chapter. A preacher is needed in your life so that you can hear the word of God in order to establish and increase your faith. The purpose of a preacher is to equip the body of Christ. We have provided the scripture Ephesians 4:11-16, which explains the various types of preachers that God has ordained—as opposed to those created by religion or man-made doctrine.

"However, when He, the Spirit of truth, has come, He will guide you into all truth; for He will not speak on His own *authority,* but whatever He hears He will speak; and He will tell you things to come." *John 16:13 NKJV*

"And He Himself gave some to be apostles, some prophets, some evangelists, and some pastors and teachers, for the equipping of the saints for the work of ministry, for the edifying of the body of Christ, till we all come to the unity of the faith and of the knowledge of the Son of God, to a perfect man, to the measure of the stature of the fullness of Christ; that we should no longer be children, tossed to and fro and carried about with every wind of doctrine, by the trickery of men, in the cunning craftiness of deceitful plotting, but, speaking the truth in love, may grow up in all things into Him who is the head—Christ— from whom the whole body, joined and knit together by what every joint supplies, according to the effective working by which every

part does its share, causes growth of the body for the edifying of itself in love." *Ephesians 4:11-16 NKJV*

"How then shall they call on Him in whom they have not believed? And how shall they believe in Him of whom they have not heard? And how shall they hear without a preacher? And how shall they preach unless they are sent? As it is written:
'How beautiful are the feet of those who preach the gospel of peace,
Who bring glad tidings of good things!'
But they have not all obeyed the gospel. For Isaiah says, 'Lord, who has believed our report?' So then faith *comes* by hearing, and hearing by the word of God." *Romans 10:14-17 NKJV*

Our prayer is that you have access to all five ministry leaders because they are the governing offices that Christ fulfilled. We know that many people may be more familiar with the offices of an Evangelist, Pastor, and Teacher, but the two offices that lay the foundation of the church are Apostles and Prophets.

"Now, therefore, you are no longer strangers and foreigners, but fellow citizens with the saints and members of the household of God, having been built on the foundation of the apostles and prophets, Jesus Christ Himself being the chief cornerstone, in whom the whole building, being fitted together, grows into a holy temple in the Lord, in whom you also are being built together for a dwelling place of God in the Spirit." *Ephesians 2:19-22 NKJV*

We are not insulting the other three five-fold ministry offices; we are substantiating the importance of Apostles and Prophets within the body of Christ. Apostles establish order in the church and build the foundation of Christ as our rock. Prophets speak, see, write, sing, and dance the heart and mind of God. They also come to set order in our lives–to destroy yokes of bondage, to call out sin, and to bring light to dark places–spiritually, naturally, and financially. Prophets strengthen, encourage, and comfort us about situations that occurred in our past, are happening in our present, or pertaining to our future.

**"Then the word of the Lord came to me, saying: 'Before I formed you in the womb I knew you; Before you were born I sanctified you; I ordained you a prophet to the nations.' Then said I: 'Ah, Lord God! Behold, I cannot speak, for I am a youth.' But the Lord said to me: 'Do not say, 'I am a youth,' For you shall go to all to whom I send you, and whatever I command you, you shall speak. Do not be afraid of their faces, For I am with you to deliver you,' says the Lord. Then the Lord put forth His hand and touched my mouth, and the Lord said to me: 'Behold, I have put My words in your mouth. See, I have this day set you over the nations and over the kingdoms, To root out and to pull down, To destroy and to throw down, To build and to plant.'" *Jeremiah 1:4-10 NKJV*

True Apostles and Prophets teach us that our foundation is Christ Jesus, and if we are rooted in Him then we can succeed and stand firm whenever attacks, trials, and storms of life come our way. They also reveal to us the mysteries of God and drive out ignorance (darkness). They launch people into their destiny so that they may fulfill it while on the earth.

Overall, a five-fold leader assists the body of Christ Jesus in knowing and understanding what God loves, and what He abhors. They clarify His desires for His sons and daughters. In order to know Him, we have to spend time with Him, and we must not solely build our relationship with Him through another person's perspective, viewpoint, or teaching.

Although the five-fold ministry leads us according to His word, we are responsible for our relationship with God. To know Him is to spend time meditating on His word, devoting time to prayer and fasting, learning how to hear His voice, and offering true praise and worship. Once we begin to know Him, we begin to know our true identity and to walk in His characteristics, because He is our Creator.

Chapter II: God's Will

As human beings, God has given us the power of free will. This means that God does not control us, and He does not make us do anything. He gives us a choice to obey His instructions or not to obey. However, *God's* will for our lives is His ultimate plan for our lives. His perfect will is tailor-made just for you. Oftentimes, we have to do things we do not desire or enjoy, but it is for our benefit and for the saving of others' lives.

It is easy to think that our desires always line up with His will for our lives, but they do not. If our desires do not line up with His written word in the Holy Bible—or prophecy, which still lines up with His written word when spoken by a human vessel—then we are committing sin due to disobedience or hesitation.

"But each one is tempted when he is drawn away by his own desires and enticed. Then, when desire has conceived, it gives birth to sin; and sin, when it is full-grown, brings forth death." *James 1:14-15 NKJV*

To sin means to do what God does not want us to do, to say or speak what God does not want us to say or speak, and to think in ways God does not want us to think. For example, God does not want us to steal and we should not love money because it is the root of all kinds of evil.

"You shall not steal." *Exodus 20:15 NKJV*

"But those who desire to be rich fall into temptation and a snare, and into many foolish and harmful lusts which drown men in destruction and perdition. For the love of money is a root of all kinds of evil, for which some have strayed from the faith in their greediness, and pierced themselves through with many sorrows." *1 Timothy 6:10 NKJV*

When we desire to have money more than we desire to have Jesus Christ, and we are willing to do anything to have money, such as stealing, we are in a position to die spiritually. We also put ourselves in a situation to die naturally, because we could be killed for trying to steal someone else's money. We only live spiritually by believing in Christ Jesus and following His instructions.

His will is obeying what He says, even when our flesh tells us to do it another way. His plan is for us to look just like Him and for us to see ourselves the way He sees us—without any distorted perspective. When He sees us, He sees not only our natural or fleshly appearances, He also sees our heart.

When our actions, hearts, and thoughts are pure, God is pleased, and He sees no faults. In addition, His will for us is to be saved and to come to the knowledge of the truth which is the word of God. We must possess the knowledge and know the fullness of who God Jehovah is. To not know all of Him is to live in darkness. To neglect a part of Him—God the Father, Jesus Christ the Son of God, and the Holy Spirit—is to be in error.

"For this is good and acceptable in the sight of God our Savior, who desires all men to be saved and to come to the knowledge of the truth. For there is one God and one Mediator between God and men, the Man Christ Jesus, who gave Himself a ransom for all, to be testified in due time." *1 Timothy 2:3-6 NKJV*

Yes, many of you are right when you say no one can see God's face and still live, which is why He gave us His Son in the flesh, Jesus Christ. Jesus Christ humbled himself, came down from heaven, and walked the earth as man to be our example.

During the thirty-three years of Jesus's life here on earth as a man, He continuously showed us how to seek after God's face and how to seek after God's will for our lives. He did so by instructing us to get into our rightful place as His sons and daughters.

"Grace to you and peace from God the Father and our Lord Jesus Christ, who gave Himself for our sins, that He might deliver us from this present evil age, according to the will of our God and Father, to whom be glory forever and ever. Amen." *Galatians 1:3-5 NKJV*

"Then He said to them all, 'If anyone desires to come after Me, let him deny himself, and take up his cross daily, and follow Me.'" *Luke 9:23 NKJV*

"And He was withdrawn from them about a stone's throw, and He knelt down and prayed, saying, 'Father, if it is Your will, take this cup away from Me; nevertheless not My will, but Yours, be done.'" *Luke 22:41-42 NKJV*

"Do not love the world or the things in the world. If anyone loves the world, the love of the Father is not in him. For all that is in the world—the lust of the flesh, the lust of the eyes, and the pride of life—is not of the Father but is of the world. And the world is passing away, and the lust of it; but he who does the will of God abides forever. *1 John 2:15-17 NKJV*

When we seek God's will for our lives, we are able to know our true identity and to be confident in who we are. Once we know that we are sons and daughters of the Most High God, we begin to walk in His character and share who He is with others.

All of us have sought after our identity by letting our pains, sufferings, fears, and lusts tell us who we are and how we should see ourselves and conduct ourselves. But it did not and does not bring fulfillment nor does it provide peace because the Prince of Peace (Jesus Christ) is not the focus and does not live in our hearts. Therefore, we can forgive and let go of those things that are behind us or that are from our past.

"Not that I have already attained, or am already perfected; but I press on, that I may lay hold of that for which Christ Jesus has also laid hold of me. Brethren, I do not count myself to have apprehended; but one thing I do, forgetting those things which are behind and reaching forward to those things which are ahead, I press toward the goal for

the prize of the upward call of God in Christ Jesus."
Philippians 3:12-1 NKJV

The way we are able to get in alignment with God's will is by submitting, worshipping, and glorifying Him in all that we do. Our heavenly Father's will is for us to be in His presence always. Being in His presence is peace, Him smiling upon you, and His angels and heaven rejoicing with singing over you.

"The Lord your God in your midst, The Mighty One, will save; He will rejoice over you with gladness, He will quiet you with His love, He will rejoice over you with singing." *Zephaniah 3:17 NKJV*

"Submit to God and be at peace with him; in this way, prosperity will come to you." *Job 22:21 NIV*

"You will keep him in perfect peace, Whose mind is stayed on You, Because he trusts in You." *Isaiah 26:3 NKJV*

"Make sure that nobody pays back wrong for wrong, but always strive to do what is good for each other and for everyone else. Rejoice always, pray continually, give thanks in all circumstances; for this is God's will for you in Christ Jesus. Do not quench the Spirit." *1 Thessalonians 5:15-19 NIV*

"A man's heart plans his way, But the Lord directs his steps." *Proverbs 16:9 NKJV*

God still speaks to this very day just as He has done since the foundation of the earth and the heavens were made. He speaks in a still small voice and God is His living and written word. God sounds like His word. Anything that is contrary to the word of God is not Him and your lifestyle should match His word.

"God is not human, that he should lie, not a human being, that he should change his mind. Does he speak and then not act? Does he promise and not fulfill?" *Numbers 23:19 NIV*

"For this reason, we also, since the day we heard it, do not cease to pray for you, and to ask that you may be filled with the knowledge of His will in all wisdom and spiritual understanding; that you may walk worthy of the Lord, fully pleasing Him, being fruitful in every good work and increasing in the knowledge of God; strengthened with all might, according to His glorious power, for all patience and longsuffering with joy; giving thanks to the Father who has qualified us to be partakers of the inheritance of the saints in the light. He has delivered us from the power of darkness and conveyed us into the kingdom of the Son of His love, in whom we have redemption through His blood, the forgiveness of sins." *Colossians 1:9-14 NKJV*

Chapter III: Healing and Deliverance

The power of God is seen through healing and deliverance, but God is not limited to this. A church not operating in the full manifestation of the Holy Spirit unfortunately will not lead the body to receive all of Christ. It will not lead each member of its congregation to be free and live as a child of God, which our Heavenly Father designed us to be. We both have encountered individuals who are either afraid when the word *deliverance* is mentioned or have no understanding of what deliverance ministry is.

We too were once blinded from this form of God's power, but as soon as we experienced it, we understood that all spirit-filled, born-again believers must continually experience healing and deliverance. This world we live in is a dirty place, and we should be able to come to the church as a well of refreshment, as a place of refuge, or as a hospital to be spiritually cleansed and set free.

"And when He had called His twelve disciples to Him, He gave them power over unclean spirits, to cast them out, and to heal all kinds of sickness and all kinds of disease." *Matthew 10:1 NKJV*

Healing and deliverance can be experienced anywhere through the Holy Spirit and angels coming upon you. In a Holy Spirit-filled gathering, healing and deliverance can take place during praise, worship, altar calls, through the laying on of hands from ministers or believers, when receiving prayer or a prophetic word, and, lastly, through good prophetic teaching (from an Apostle, Prophet, or Teacher). Healing and deliverance are not confined to the four walls of a church. The only thing the Lord requires is that we are willing to let His word minister to us and that we hold on to it so it can transform us.

If you think you do not need healing or deliverance, then you absolutely have a self-righteous spirit operating in your life. For we do not know what we need, but the Father always knows what we are in need of when it comes to healing and deliverance from the spirit realm. Let's define healing and deliverance so that we are clear on the many ways in which they can show up in our lives.

Healing is to make one healthy, whole, or sound; restore to health; free from illness or disease, torment, or bondage.

Deliverance is salvation, liberty, rescue, or cleansing. In ministry, it refers to cleansing a person from evil spirits/demons, which cause problems to manifest in their life as a result of the demonic presences oppressing a person's life.

Healing and deliverance manifest spiritually, naturally, and financially. Examples of healing and deliverance include, but are not limited to, the following examples.
- Spiritually healed and delivered from generational curses, family curses, ancestral spirits hindering

success, demonic spirits, thoughts, strongholds, diseases, illnesses, and conditions

- Naturally healed and delivered to new geographical locations, new homes, new cars, pregnancy in barren wombs, beginning ministry, access to higher education, food, businesses, and writing books; healing from anatomical, physiological, and psychological diseases, illnesses, and conditions

- Financially healed and delivered to start giving tithes/offerings/seeds/first fruits/vows, having multiple bank accounts, debt cancellation, credit score increase, salary increase, career promotions, multiple streams of income, wealth, and resource opportunities.

The symptoms of a process of deliverance include crying, yelling, screaming, coughing or vomiting, spitting up phlegm, and nasal discharge of phlegm exiting the body. Spirits seek to take root living in our bodies. Their goal is to find a human (or house) to dwell in with the hope of tormenting us spiritually, naturally, and financially.

"When an unclean spirit goes out of a man, he goes through dry places, seeking rest; and finding none, he says, 'I will return to my house from which I came.' And when he comes, he finds *it* swept and put in order. Then he goes and takes with *him* seven other spirits more wicked than himself, and they enter and dwell there, and the last *state* of that man is worse than the first." *Luke 11:24-26 NKJV*

Considering the previous text from Luke 11, once our house (or body) is delivered, swept clean, and put in order from one unclean spirit, we must continue to keep ourselves cleansed and in order. If not, that one unclean spirit seeks and attempts to bring in seven more wicked spirits back to us—plotting to make our condition worse than it was. A continual experience of healing and deliverance within ourselves and witnessing it take place in the lives of others is a miraculous lifestyle that our Father in heaven wants us to have as His sons and daughters.

"Beloved, I pray that you may prosper in all things and be in health, just as your soul prospers." *3 John 1:2 NKJV*

Everything is spiritual. Healing and deliverance are meant to destroy the root of the toxic spirits living in your heart and soul. Every level of healing and deliverance takes us higher in the spirit realm with heaven backing us. Once we ascend higher in the spiritual realm, we never fight the same demons or spirits again.

There are many spirits that are not of God that the enemy tries to use to keep us in bondage and separated from God and from God's plans for our lives. Out of all of the demonic spirits, there are three major spirits that the enemy tries to release in order to overtake us. They are the spirit of rejection, the spirit of abandonment, and the spirit of orphanhood. These spirits usually take hold when we are children, and they linger throughout adulthood if not addressed and cast out of us.

The spirit of rejection occurs when a person or group of people excludes an individual and refuses to acknowledge or accept them, refusing to believe someone or something.

The spirit of abandonment takes hold when a person or group deserts someone—never to return.

The spirit of orphanhood occurs when a child has lost both parents through death or abandonment; it also manifests in a child that is raised with a parent's physical presence but emotional absence and without a protective spiritual covering.

We can identify these spirits with the help of the Holy Spirit. The Holy Spirit is our counselor and teacher. He helps us discern all things since everything is spiritual. These three spirits also cause branches to grow, birthing other spirits within our lives. Therefore, when they are not identified and cast out, the manifestation of other demonic spirits fights to enter with a motive to wreak havoc.

Some of the other ungodly spirits that are manifested by way of the three primary spirits are fear, doubt, lust, perversion, pride, rebellion, resentment, vanity, arrogance, depression, regret, shame, guilt, bitterness, envy, greed, drunkenness, addiction, profanity, anger, sexual immorality, fornication, sorcery, unforgiveness, hesitancy, and double-mindedness—just to name a few.

We cannot stress enough that Jesus Christ is a healer and a deliverer, and we all have access to know Him as such. To not know this grace of God's power will have us bound in repeated cycles of experiencing torment and hell. Negative thoughts, feelings, and emotions we feel are all spiritual beings, and the battlefield is within our minds.

Thoughts are ideas or opinions produced by thinking or a reflection of what is in one's heart.

Feelings are beliefs, conscious or vague awareness, and pleasurable or painful perceptions.

Emotions are instinctive feelings as distinguished from reasoning or knowledge—a subjective state of mind that predisposes us to react a certain way.

Therefore, once we become born-again believers, healing and deliverance are our portions. Healing and deliverance take place spiritually, naturally, and financially. Sometimes they occur instantly, while at other times they take place gradually. The important thing here is that, whether instant or gradual, healing and deliverance are possible for each and every one of us.

The ways that we can get delivered and healed from these spirits are by a minister speaking the word of God to us, through reading the Holy Bible with the wisdom of God, increasing our spiritual understanding, and continuing to allow Christ to dwell within our hearts. When He's in our hearts, we stop viewing things from a broken perspective. We do not hold on to past pain and suffering, and we do not allow things to bother us as they once did. We come to possess peace, and Jesus is that peace. Therefore, peace means victory!

We have provided a few scriptures that will aid you in understanding the power of healing and deliverance. Knowing Jesus and believing in the written word of God is our only resource for defeating the enemy. The word tells us who we are and, most importantly, whose we are!

"This I say, therefore, and testify in the Lord, that you should no longer walk as the rest of the Gentiles walk, in the futility of their mind, having their understanding darkened, being alienated from the life of God, because of the ignorance that is in them, because of the blindness of their heart; who, being past feeling, have given themselves over to lewdness, to work all uncleanness with greediness. But you have not so learned Christ, if indeed you have heard Him and have been taught by Him, as the truth is in Jesus: that you put off, concerning your former conduct, the old man which grows corrupt according to the deceitful lusts, and be renewed in the spirit of your mind, and that you put on the new man which was created according to God, in true righteousness and holiness." *Ephesians 4:17-24 NKJV*

"For He, Himself has said, 'I will never leave you nor forsake you.'" *Hebrews 13:5 NKJV*

"Blessed be the God and Father of our Lord Jesus Christ, who has blessed us with every spiritual blessing in the

heavenly places in Christ, just as He chose us in Him before the foundation of the world, that we should be holy and without blame before Him in love, having predestined us to adoption as sons by Jesus Christ to Himself, according to the good pleasure of His will, to the praise of the glory of His grace, by which He made us accepted in the Beloved." *Ephesians 1:3-6 NKJV*

"Therefore, brethren, we are debtors—not to the flesh, to live according to the flesh. For if you live according to the flesh you will die; but if by the Spirit you put to death the deeds of the body, you will live. For as many as are led by the Spirit of God, these are sons of God. For you did not receive the spirit of bondage again to fear, but you received the Spirit of adoption by whom we cry out, "Abba, Father." The Spirit Himself bears witness with our spirit that we are children of God, and if children, then heirs—heirs of God and joint-heirs with Christ, if indeed we suffer with Him, that we may also be glorified together." *Romans 8:12-17 NKJV*

"Assuredly, I say to you, whatever you bind on earth will be bound in heaven, and whatever you loose on earth will be loosed in heaven." *Matthew 18:18 NKJV*

"He who believes and is baptized will be saved, but he who does not believe will be condemned. And these signs will follow those who believe: In my name, they will cast out demons; they will speak with new tongues; they will take up serpents; and if they drink anything deadly, it will by no means hurt them; they will lay hands on the sick, and they will recover." *Mark 16: 16-18 NKJV*

"Shake yourself from the dust, arise; Sit down, O Jerusalem! Loose yourself from the bonds of your neck, O captive daughter of Zion!" *Isaiah 52:2 NKJV*

"For as he thinks in his heart, so is he." *Proverbs 23:7 NKJV*

"...that He might present her to Himself a glorious church, not having spot or wrinkle or any such thing, but that she should be holy and without blemish." *Ephesians 5:27 NKJV*

"Therefore if the Son makes you free, you shall be free indeed." *John 8:36 NKJV*

"Then Jesus said to those Jews who believed Him, 'If you abide in My word, you are My disciples indeed. And you shall know the truth, and the truth shall make you free.'" *John 8:31-32 NKJV*

"...And by His stripes, we are healed." *Isaiah 53:5 NKJV*

Chapter IV: Fix Your Environment

Your environment matters! To live, grow, and learn God's perfect will or plan for your life, an important principle to follow is to monitor the company you keep and change your environment when necessary. The three realms of most individuals' social environments are 1) family and friends, 2) coworkers and/or classmates, and 3) church family.

The enemy likes to attack us in these areas because this is where most people know us from a natural and close-knit perspective. If we experience any level of battle here and have a continuous endless cycle of friction, then we can become defeated if we do not realize that this is where Satan likes to attack us the most.

From a biblical perspective on social environments, King Solomon (who is the wisest man filled with God's wisdom) speaks about the importance of who is around you. King Solomon gives us the wise proverbs about the instructions of what makes a man or woman of God wise and what constitutes a foolish man or woman **(See Proverbs 9)**.

We all know the cliché saying "sticks and stones may break my bones, but words will never hurt me," right? This is absolutely wrong. Many people's suffering from their childhood and through their entire adult life comes from the words (spirits) that were spoken to them or over them. In fact, *most* feelings of pain, hurt, rejection, and unbelief are caused by words that others have spoken.

Words linger and can be sown as seeds for good or evil. Words are spirits, which means they can cause life or death to occur. These spirits can run deeply through bloodlines, leading to generational curses or strongholds wanting to prevent the releasing of God's blessings and promises upon one's life.

"Death and life are in the power of the tongue, And those who love it will eat its fruit." *Proverbs 18:21 NKJV*

The environments we are born into and naturally raised in are ordained before we were formed in our mother's womb. This presents a challenge for many of us seeking to be delivered into a new environment. We must find family (spiritual leaders) and discover our place in God's plan in order to fulfill our destiny. The truth is, some family, friends, and loved ones can be dream-killers. However, we will examine how to learn when it is the appropriate time or season to share provisions from the Lord.

Most loved ones do not kill or deny our goals intentionally, but the words they speak may discourage us, cause emotional hurt, or lead to a breakdown in communication. These negative outcomes are exactly what the enemy wants. The enemy wants to stifle the fulfillment of your vision that is meant to impact 10s, 100s, or 1000s of lives while here on the earth through small irritations, rejections, and disagreements.

God loves family, and it has been His plan for us to have that structured support system since the very beginning. We know that many people may not have had their natural mothers and fathers in their lives, or some may have had their parents not present the way a child would have liked for them to be. The enemy attempts to weaponize these circumstances to hinder God's children from manifesting the Lord's provisions throughout adulthood.

Therefore, we must understand that the spirits of rejection, abandonment, and orphanhood try to come in at an early age as we are forming the structure in our mind of what a family design looks and feels like. Although our natural families may not be the way we would like for them to be, God knew who needed to birth us and how they were going to raise us or not raise us so we can bring glory to His name. Every situation that appears broken to the untrained eye is just a future opportunity to share with others what the Lord has done and will do.

As you grow in Christ, the dynamic of most relationships will begin to change. People will either stay or drift apart instantly due to your decision to live for Christ and give up the sinful nature that the relationships were founded upon. We both have had many friendships built on shallow ground. God's love and Jesus Christ were not the foundation of it, and we ultimately had to release those connections. Most of our connections were based on common interests such as education, partying, gossip, and lustful desires. These relationships wasted time and drained us spiritually.

One prayer that we continuously pray is: *Lord, please remove anyone that does not need to be in our lives in order to fulfill your will. For those that are meant to be for a season or for a lifetime, let it be revealed with no love lost.* The relationships that were no longer necessary, we did not end on negative terms. The communication either ceased peacefully, or, after we shared what the Lord has done for us, is doing for us, and what He could do for them, they never responded.

We can never forget that to be a born-again believer means to have a community and a social life. As we have said, the Lord loves family—no matter if it's your natural family or your spiritual family. Therefore, being a proclaimed loner or an introvert is not what we are suggesting you do to improve your social circle. *Agape* relationships should be established by the spirit of truth. He will guide you into knowing who should stay around, who should be removed, or who should be added.

Agape love refers to a pure, willful, or sacrificial love.

We all need to have a form or structure of family (naturally or spiritually), a supportive group of people, or a team that reflects who we are and are striving to become. A lot of people in this world have had relationships (romantic or non-romantic) that have left them feeling rejected, hurt, and lacking trust towards new or healthy heaven-sent relationships. If we allow it, the past can sabotage the future before it even starts.

When you truly give yourself to God completely and you decide to live righteously and holy, you will not become a partaker in others' sins. There is often no ill intent or even a solid reason why communication has stopped with certain individuals, but when God brings you into a new dimension of trust with Him, you have to remove those who are not connected to your destiny. Having the wrong associations can be a hindrance to your peace or even a bad influence on you spiritually, naturally, and financially.

For example, in the book of Job **(See Job 2)**, all of Job's friends had good intentions, but all of his friends gave him bad counsel. We have been there. The enemy will try to attack you through those close to you by having them plant negative, discouraging seeds (words). Sometimes, those who plant negative seeds are unaware of what they are doing, which is why the gift of discerning of spirits is needed.

Changing your environment may be an active choice or done spiritually without any physical work. We are not saying that all the people in your life are bad for you, but you have to become consciously aware of who is connected to you and determine the depth of the relationship. An individual could be there for an ordained season, a lesson, or a lifelong companionship. When you have the right environment, distractions become minimized, you do not waste time because you know you have a purpose and a destiny to fulfill before your time runs out on the earth.

Having a small intimate group of people that you can fellowship with while either in or outside of the church is needed. Not only should the group members be your friends but you all can be each other's prayer partners, fighting in intercession spiritually for endless breakthroughs and victories.

"Again, truly I tell you that if two of you on earth agree about anything they ask for, it will be done for them by my

Father in heaven. For where two or three gather in my name, there am I with them." *Matthew 18:19-20 NKJV*

An example in the Bible that depicts being a product of one's environment is how Saul is chosen and anointed as king over Israel. This is one of our favorite texts in scripture **(1 Samuel 9 and 1 Samuel 10).** The prophet Samuel is speaking the word of the Lord to Saul, giving him instructions and telling him what will happen when he comes into the company of the prophets:

"Then you shall go on forward from there and come to the terebinth tree of Tabor. There, three men going up to God at Bethel will meet you, one carrying three young goats, another carrying three loaves of bread, and another carrying a skin of wine. And they will greet you and give you two loaves of bread, which you shall receive from their hands. After that, you shall come to the hill of God where the Philistine garrison is. And it will happen, when you have come there to the city, that you will meet a group of prophets coming down from the high place with a stringed instrument, a tambourine, a flute, and a harp before them; and they will be prophesying. Then the Spirit of the Lord will come upon you, and you will prophesy with them and be turned into another man. And let it be, when these signs come to you, that you do as the occasion demands; for God is with you. You shall go down before me to Gilgal; surely I will come down to you to offer burnt offerings and make sacrifices of peace offerings. Seven days you shall wait, till I come to you and show you what you should do. So it was when he had turned his back to go from Samuel, that God gave him another heart; and all those signs came

to pass that day. When they came there to the hill, there was a group of prophets to meet him; then the Spirit of God came upon him, and he prophesied among them. And it happened when all who knew him formerly saw that he indeed prophesied among the prophets, that the people said to one another, 'What is this that has come upon the son of Kish? Is Saul also among the prophets?'" *1 Samuel 10:3-11 NKJV*

Saul received impartation, leading to the beginning of his reign as king for the children of Israel.

Impartation is the transmission of information, the giving and receiving of spiritual gifts, blessings, healing, revelation, and baptism in the Holy Spirit for the work of a ministry.

With this resource from Abba, it is the transference of these "gifts" from one man or woman of God to another activating what is lying dormant inside. We are so grateful for the apostolic and prophetic ministry because it is so powerful and necessary for the building of God's kingdom on the earth. The anointing of this ministry destroys yokes of bondage, curses, and allows the Holy Spirit to change your environment, launching you into success.

Remaining confident in yourself, never letting anyone discourage you from where you know you are called to, and the people you are called to. Some people are assigned by the enemy into our lives to be destiny-assassins, weighing you down with negative commentary that drains your progress and leads to negative thought patterns or habits.

The Holy Spirit as our helper gives us insight on how to deal with such assignments and how to destroy all forms of destruction. However, when the right environment is created for you, you will do what feeds you spiritually, take heed to it, and be in perfect peace. Your environment is so imperative to your spiritual growth, even when it comes down to what you listen to and what you watch.

What we hear and see ministers to our souls. This includes music, books, articles, social media, videos, and television. The key part of the word entertainment is *enter.* All of these components of entertainment have a source, and we need to know what source we are feeding our spirit-man. Again, spirits travel through sounds, words, or images that are seeds planted and watered in our hearts. Whatever is planted in our hearts we will ponder on it, speak it, or react according to it.

We must be aware of our doors and gates (eyes, ears, etc.) that can open us up to unclean, perverted, and evil spirits. Therefore, always allow and make God the Father, His Son Jesus Christ, and the Holy Spirit your door and gatekeeper.

"Above all else, guard your heart, for everything you do flows from it." *Proverbs 4:23 NIV*

"My son, do not forget my teaching, but keep my commands in your heart, for they will prolong your life many years and bring you peace and prosperity." *Proverbs 3:1-2 NIV*

If you are in need of a few artists and creatives to listen to, we have listed a few of them below. They have helped reshape our thinking and, most importantly, have led us to Christ.

Briana Babineaux
Bryann Trejo & Monica Trejo (Kingdom Muzic)
Isabel Davis
Jonathan McReynolds
Johnathan Traylor
Marv Rogers
Maverick City
Micah Tyler
Tauren Wells
Todd Dulaney
Travis Greene
We Will Worship
Young Bro

Chapter V: The Fight for The Future

The fight for the future is significant and is based upon Godly wisdom. Having God's spirit of wisdom is all about our future. We are not talking about seeking advice from family, friends, podcasts, and celebrities. There are thousands of self-help books, life coaches, and motivational speakers, but you have to decide where true instruction and insight comes from. We are not saying that these things are bad, but it is most important that all of us learn how to hear from the author of creation, which is God.

The seven spirits of God are what all of us should be operating in daily as believers in Jesus Christ.

"The Spirit of the Lord shall rest upon Him, the spirit of wisdom and understanding, the spirit of counsel and might, the spirit of knowledge, and of the fear of the Lord." *Isaiah 11:2 NKJV*

Without the spirit of wisdom, you are a fool making decisions concerning your life blindly while here on the earth. To live blindly is to follow the world's wisdom using your emotions and feelings, not praying to hear from the Lord before doing or committing to something. Again, we both have been there.

Will you make mistakes as a born-again believer? The answer is, 100% yes! However, with the spirit of wisdom operating in your life, she will teach you, guide you, and instruct you on what you ought to do to limit those mistakes–if you seek her.

Wisdom is a female spirit because she has the authority to create and produce wealth in our lives. She has been with God from the very beginning, and she created the foundation of the earth.

"Tune your ears to wisdom, and concentrate on understanding. Cry out for insight, and ask for understanding. Search for them as you would for silver; seek them like hidden treasures. Then you will understand what it means to fear the LORD, and you will gain knowledge of God. For the LORD grants wisdom! From his mouth come knowledge and understanding. He grants a treasure of common sense to the honest. He is a shield to those who walk with integrity. He guards the paths of the just and protects those who are faithful to him. Then you will understand what is right, just, and fair, and you will find the right way to go. For wisdom will enter your heart, and knowledge will fill you with joy. Wise choices will watch over you. Understanding will keep you safe. Wisdom will save you from evil people, from those whose words are twisted." *Proverbs 2:2-12 NLT*

"Therefore, 'If anyone lacks wisdom, let him ask of God, who gives to all liberally and without reproach, and it will be given to him.'" *James 1:5 NKJV*

As a born-again believer, you should know the five books of wisdom that assist us with our daily struggles and human experiences: Job, Psalms, Proverbs, Ecclesiastes, and Song of Solomon. However, we must warn you from experience that you cannot jump right into these books without a humble and teachable spirit ready to accept wisdom. It will be challenging to receive and digest what the Holy Spirit is saying, so please take your time with her, get to know her, and love her.

Everyone is assigned a destiny for their life while down here on earth. Destiny is God's plan for your life to complete His perfect will. Being saved, along with living holy and righteous will get you into heaven, but it is not all that our Heavenly Father wants for us. He has a purpose and a calling for each and every one of us to complete. We all have work to do that glorifies Him and draws men unto Him if we lift Him up.

Sometimes we do not always know our purpose, so having a true prophet in our life, and seeking Godly counsel and wisdom is imperative. Once you know your purpose and it lines up with the word of God, because Jesus Christ is the word and His word sounds like Him, you can never be led in the wrong direction.

Living and working out your purpose in the perfect will of God requires us to step out in faith. It may not be a pleasant or comfortable feeling. As Christians, we often don't talk enough about the hard decision to fully let go and let the Lord lead us. Letting our Lord Jesus Christ lead is submission and honor. With submission comes rebuking and correction, but a wise man loves to be corrected. He or she will see many victories in their life spiritually, naturally, and financially.

"A wise son heeds his father's instruction, but a scoffer does not listen to rebuke." *Proverbs 13:1 NKJV*

We both had to be introduced to Godly wisdom at the age of 26. Since we have invited her into our lives, she has protected us from many situations that the enemy crafted. We both have had several verbal opportunities to work for others and be a boost to their companies, but the Holy Spirit convicted us and spoke to us to turn the offers down. Giving in would have had us drawn completely outside of every prophecy and God's word concerning us.

We thank God we never moved forward or invited the emotions and cunning ways that the enemy tried to use to pull us into projects that were not God's perfect will for us. We are not saying that the individuals involved were bad people, they were just vessels that the enemy attempted to use by way of words (spirits) to distract us. We would have been operating in our permissive will of the flesh and instant gratification.

In the closing of this book, we want to leave you with a few scriptures and short prayers to let you know that God loves you and we love you. We speak peace to your heart and mind and we pray that you develop a Christian walk that strengthens and increases your relationship with the Lord. We pray for success and blessings as you have taken the time to invest in your spirit-man's activation.

"What do you want me to do for you? Jesus asked him." *Mark 10:51 NIV*

"Therefore, if anyone is in Christ, he is a new creation; old things have passed away; behold, all things have become new." *2 Corinthians 5:17 NKJV*

"Casting down imaginations, and every high thing that exalteth itself against the knowledge of God, and bringing into captivity every thought to the obedience of Christ." *2 Corinthians 10:5 KJV*

"Now to Him who is able to do exceedingly abundantly above all that we ask or think, according to the power that works in us, to Him be glory in the church by Christ Jesus to all generations, forever and ever. Amen." *Ephesians 3:20-21 NKJV*

Prayer

Dear Lord, you know the circumstances, conditions, and situations that I am in, and only you can deliver me from it. Help me to lean on you and not my own understanding. I give up my thoughts, desires, and passions. I give you, who is knowing of all things, complete authority to guide my life.

Prayer

*There is no need for me to fear or to have doubt when I know Jesus Christ is going with me. **"There is no fear in love; but perfect love casts out fear, because fear involves torment. But he who fears has not been made perfect in love." 1 John 4:18 KJV***

Prayer

Lord, teach me to remain victorious as I fight the good fight and to stay in a place of prayer and repentance along with deliverance and healing. In Jesus's name, Amen!

About the Authors

Doctors Ashley and Amber Goodman are a dynamic duo of emerging Evangelists. Their church home for spiritual training and equipping is Heaven to Earth Worship Center. As a result of their upbringing, academics and athletics have molded these two into the leaders they are today. Both received full scholarships to play basketball in addition to receiving academic scholarships.

After basketball concluded, their vision was set to become doctors of pharmacy. Their faith in Jesus Christ, along with a love for the apostolic and prophetic, has led them to become five-fold ministers and to further their education within the fields of public health and business administration.

As growing figureheads in healthcare with a passion for full-time ministry, they are determined to influence the quality of healthcare delivery and systems for generations to come. With this spiritual mandate, both aspire to bring light to those who are in darkness, helping others discover salvation and their place in God's perfect will. Drs. Ashley and Amber plan to continue imparting revelations of the Lord through the spirits of knowledge, wisdom, and counsel.

Acknowledgments

We acknowledge our lovely parents, Dr. Carl Goodman & Jacqueline Goodman; our spiritual parents and Overseer, Prophet Daniel Powell, Sr. & Prophetess Esther Powell; our church home, Heaven to Earth Worship Center, Faith & Works Outreach Ministries; our Chief Apostle, Kathy Kinchen & K.K. Ministries; and everyone who wants to be set free and made whole through our Lord Jesus Christ.

Made in the USA
Middletown, DE
11 April 2022

64028196R00031